How to Make a Good Confession

Also available from
Sophia Institute Press®
by John A. Kane:

Transforming Your Life Through the Eucharist

The School of Mary

Six Lessons for Life from the School of the Cross

John A. Kane

How to Make a Good Confession

A Pocket Guide to Reconciliation with God

SOPHIA INSTITUTE PRESS®
Manchester, New Hampshire

How to Make a Good Confession was originally published in 1943 by St. Anthony Guild Press, Paterson, New Jersey, as *The School of Repentance*. In 1999, Sophia Institute Press published a paperback edition entitled *Conquering Your Sins with Heartfelt Repentance*, which contained minor editorial revisions to the original text. This 2001 reprint of *Conquering Your Sins with Heartfelt Repentance* includes an introduction, revised chapter titles, and an appendix on how to make a good confession.

Printed in the United States of America

Sophia Institute Press®
Box 5284, Manchester, NH 03108
1-800-888-9344
www.sophiainstitute.com

Nihil Obstat: Henry Zolzer, *Censor librorum*
Imprimatur: Thomas H. McLaughlin, Bishop of Paterson
February 25, 1943

Library of Congress Cataloging-in-Publication Data

Kane, John A., 1883-
How to make a good confession / John A. Kane.
p. cm.
Rev. ed. of: Conquering your sins with heartfelt repentance. 1999.
Includes bibliographical references.
ISBN 1-928832-29-6 (pbk.)
1. Confession — Catholic Church. 2. Repentance. 3. Sin. 4. Christian life — Catholic authors. I. Kane, John A., 1883- Conquering your sins with heartfelt repentance. II. Title.

BX2265.2.K36 2001
264'.020862 — dc21 2001020106

22nd printing

Contents

Editor's note: The biblical references in the following pages are taken from the Douay-Rheims edition and the Revised Standard Version (RSV), Catholic Edition, of the Old and New Testaments. Where applicable, quotations from the Douay-Rheims edition have been cross-referenced with the differing enumeration in the RSV, using the following symbol: (RSV =).

Introduction

Our Lord instituted the sacrament of Penance for the forgiveness of our sins and for our reconciliation with God. But a good confession brings us more than forgiveness of our sins; it also provides us with a powerful, grace-filled means to *overcome* sins.

To ensure that you receive the greatest spiritual benefit from Confession, this book gives you the tools you need to make a good confession: a step-by-step guide through of the rite itself, as well as a detailed list of questions to help you make a good examination of conscience beforehand.

But that information you can find in many other books.

This book goes deeper, showing you how a good confession involves much more than what you do during those few moments you spend in the confessional.

To make a truly good confession, you must have developed — before you enter the confessional — those attitudes of mind and habits of soul that enable you to identify your sins (even hidden ones), to be sorry for them, and to do penance.

This book shows you how to acquire these soul-restoring attitudes of mind and soul so that you will be truly prepared when you enter the confessional, and so that God's manifold graces will flood your soul as you leave it.

How to Make a Good Confession

Chapter One

Cultivate true contrition

"For the sorrow that is
according to God worketh penance,
steadfast unto salvation."

2 Corinthians 7:10

The end of sorrow, both natural and supernatural, is correction, change. Supernatural sorrow must wean the soul from sin and turn it to God; it must, in other words, work repentance, for to repent is to change. The punishment of sin is meant to deter from sin. It is first corrective and then penal.

The child who gorges on sweets will become sick, and the man who washes his hands in scalding water will be burned, because physical laws infallibly enforce their own application. Too intense heat will always burn, and too many sweets will always sicken; hence, neither child nor man will be likely to forget the lesson taught by adversity.

Moral lessons inculcated by the dire effects of sin do not impress themselves upon us so directly, although they are just as efficacious. The first chastisement inflicted by a schoolmaster upon a recalcitrant pupil is corrective, because it constitutes a warning. It becomes penal as often afterward as it must be repeated because of repetition of the misdemeanor.

Sorrow, therefore, is a divine power when it restrains the soul from sin; in short, when it "worketh penance, steadfast unto salvation." The soul honestly appraising its past sins and their consequences cannot but be deeply touched with a sorrow prolific of perennial penitence. Holy Scripture insists on lifelong repentance. "Blessed is the man that feareth the Lord."[1] "With fear and trembling work out your salvation."[2] "Be you humbled under the mighty hand of God, that He may exalt you in the time of visitation."[3] "The sorrow that is according to God worketh penance, steadfast unto salvation." "Converse in fear during the time of your sojourning here."[4] "He that humbleth himself shall be exalted."[5]

One thought underlies all these texts; they express one dominant truth. And this momentously significant verity that comes out of them all is the idea of constant

[1] Ps. 111:1 (RSV = Ps. 112:1).

[2] Phil. 2:12.

[3] 1 Pet. 5:6.

[4] 1 Pet. 1:17.

[5] Luke 18:14.

repentance. For what are sorrow, humiliation, fear, and trembling but emanations of a deep and lasting realization of sin? They are at once the most becoming livery and the most powerful panoply of penitents, and their striking feature is their enduring character.

An inquiry into the cause of penitence reveals the same truth. Penitence is born of a consciousness of sin, and a consciousness of sin deepens with the passing of life. Repentance, therefore, intensifies as we grow older. This progressive development that we experience of the knowledge of sin is seen also in Sacred Scripture. As in ourselves, so in the Bible, the depths of sin are only gradually unfolded.

In a most remarkably simple way, the Scriptures describe the first sin. It is spoken of as an act of little moment despite the far-reaching and appalling effects of its commission. "She took of the fruit thereof and did eat, and gave to her husband who did eat."[6] The sacred writer manifests no surprise at human or divine issues, because he is revealing the God who, since He cannot change, beholds all things with infinite calm and eternal equanimity.

[6] Gen. 3:6.

Besides, the Old Testament treats of sin as affecting man socially rather than individually. The anger of God kindled by it and evoking His terrible chastisements, the harrowing effects produced by it in the world, its diffusively virulent nature, its antagonism to God — these unspeakable consequences are stressed rather than the nature of sin in itself and its effect upon man's soul.

The social aspect of sin likewise forms the burden of the Ten Commandments. The greater part of the Gospels themselves deals only with the external results of sin: its hideous deformity, its hateful selfishness, as contrasted with God's infinite love and His eternal beneficence.

Even more graphically than the books of the Old Testament do the Gospels describe these outward effects, because the light of God's incarnate presence is focused upon them. Only in the letters of the apostles, especially those of St. Paul, is the nature of sin thoroughly analyzed, its intrinsic malice clearly shown, and its deadly effect upon man's soul brought to light.

"I see," says the great apostle, "another law in my members fighting against the law of my mind, and captivating me in the law of sin that is in my members."[7]

[7] Rom. 7:23.

Again, he says: "I do not that good which I will, but the evil which I hate."[8] And again: "The flesh lusteth against the spirit, and the spirit against the flesh, for these are contrary one to another; so that you do not the things that you would."[9]

St. John comprehends all sin in "the concupiscence of the flesh, the concupiscence of the eyes, and the pride of life."[10]

Just as man's disobedience is first simply stated, and its external effect and internal malice afterward vividly described, in the same progressive manner does sin reveal itself to the soul. The commission of the first actual sin is a mere insignificant commonplace, inspiring no reasonable shame or analysis of its cause nor any deep realization of its full enormity. As we grow older, we begin to feel the actual consequences of sin, the evils flowing from it that afflict us and those we love. Gradually the knowledge of its real nature, the secret disorder wrought by it, and the ruin and desolation that it brings into the soul unfold themselves to the mind.

[8] Rom. 7:15.

[9] Gal. 5:17.

[10] 1 John 2:16.

As the years pass, this inward working of sin becomes more vivid, more terrible. It deepens more and more as the end of life approaches; and at the hour of death, even when our lips have been purpled and our souls washed with the blood of our God, even then, just because of the soul's brilliant spiritual beauty, sin becomes all the more foul and ugly. Since, therefore, the keenness of the sense of sin measures the depth of repentance, penitence must grow with advancing years.

Bearing in mind this truth, who can understand the soul's consciousness of sin after death? Then indeed, in the full blaze and radiant splendor of eternal justice, vice will appear ineffably hideous, while the appraisal of sin will be deepest precisely when the soul, after its complete purification in Purgatory, wings its flight to the eternal embrace of its God.

The momentous truth of the need of lifelong reparation for sin is exemplified in the three terms which Holy Scripture uses to denote penitence: *conversion*, *repentance*, and *contrition*; and each may signify either a transitory act or a perennial state. As separate acts, they are like the roots of giant oaks and pines, which often rise to the surface, only to return beneath it and deepen their growth. The act of penitence mounts to the surface in currents of feeling, while the state of penitence ever deepens below. But conversion, contrition, and repentance all indicate a perpetual progressiveness, a state of soul never becoming absolutely perfect, but constantly growing with advancing years.

Conversion is, literally, a turning — the turning of the soul and all its faculties from sin to complete identification with the will of God.

Contrition also intensifies as life progresses. It is unlike attrition, which (from the Latin *attero*) means only a passing bruising of the soul inspired by the thought of the loss of Heaven, the eternal punishment of sin, or the malice of sin in itself. Contrition (from the Latin *contero*, which means to rub and grind down the whole body) is a wounding of the entire soul, making it thereby sensitively tender and impressionable. It is born of pure love of God for His own sake.

Repentance (from the Greek *metanoia*) is the mind itself changed and transformed. It is the supernatural conquering the natural. It is the assumption of the spirit of Christ according to the words of St. Paul: "Let this mind be in you which was also in Christ Jesus."[11]

[11] Phil. 2:5.

Thus it is evident that penitence, in its entirety, is perennial. It has not always the same quality, however. It assumes different phases, and in this respect it is like a lifelong grief. The first outburst of sorrow will subside. The wilderness of desolation will bloom again with fragrant flowers. In resignation to the divine will, the soul will be flooded with light, peace, and joy. Then will it glory in the consciousness that it is suffering with Christ. Its sorrow is now more abiding; it has taken root in the very depths of the soul's consciousness; it clings to the soul far more tenaciously than the first convulsive paroxysm of grief. Without any external evidence, sorrow has silently transfigured the soul's life, uniting it more fully, more intimately, more consciously with its God. A calm and permanent sorrow, which at first terrorized the soul, now lovingly embraces it and gradually sinks into its extreme depths, while externally there may have been no sign of its existence.

Penitence acts likewise. The initial expression of grief will cease; the tears will by degrees diminish; the wound inflicted by sin will gradually close. The first instinctive feelings of disappointment with self, loathing, and remorse will quiet down and become more reasonable. But the awful realization of the soul's spiritual state, the one all-absorbing thought of the horror of sin, will be more vivid, immeasurably truer, and will assume a more disciplined form. And as the interior spirit of repentance grows and at the same time becomes calmer, gentler, and more enlightened, the sense of the meaning of sin will intensify, and the thought of God's mercy to sinners will rouse the soul's hope and dispel the mists and shadows of that first anguish of somewhat unreasonable sorrow and remorse. The soul's powers, thus renewed, will now live their life in the eternal sunshine of the mercy and love of God.

To the superficial observer, repentance may then appear to have ceased. It has, however, only sunk deeper into the soul. It is invisible because it has rooted itself in the soul's innermost being. Its very hiddenness robs it of all external assertiveness. It has thoroughly intermingled with the soul's deepest source of life, like food completely assimilated by the body. It has made the soul far more responsive to grace; it has sensitized the soul's faculties; it has silently and secretly developed the soul's realization of God's most wondrous prerogative: mercy; it has bound the soul irrevocably to Christ and revived the soul's adoption by Him who "desires not the death of the wicked, but that the wicked turn from his way and live,"[12] and thus it has become the impetus of the soul's advancement in virtue, the inspiration of its power for good, and its daily shield in its struggle for eternal life.

The soul now serves God more freely and more lovingly because it realizes the contrast between its past sinfulness and its present holiness, and the marvelous way in which the mercy of God has effected the change. This perennial penitential state, because of its hidden and profound depth, is all the more real. It is a creature of intelligence and calm confidence, not of blind instinct and selfish sorrow for sin. It transcends the natural because it is born of faith.

A pious legend states that even to the day of his martyrdom, St. Peter, whenever he heard the crowing of the cock, wept anew. The mighty flood of sorrow still flowed that broke forth within him when, on the night of his denial, he went out and wept bitterly.[13] In his epistles, penitence is not mentioned. But no other letters are more replete with soul-stirring pleas for humility, watchfulness, and fear.

[12] Cf. Ezek. 33:11.

[13] Matt. 26:75.

"Be ye subject, therefore," he says, "to every human creature for God's sake."[14] "In like manner, ye young men, be subject to the ancients. . . . Insinuate humility one to another, for God resisteth the proud, but to the humble He giveth grace. Be you humbled, therefore, under the mighty hand of God, that He may exalt you in the time of visitation, casting all your care upon Him, for He hath care of you. Be sober and watch, because your adversary the Devil, as a roaring lion, goeth about seeking whom he may devour."[15] "Be prudent therefore, and watch in prayers."[16] "Fear God."[17] "Converse in fear during the time of your sojourning here."

St. Paul's letters, on the contrary, are striking for their tone of repentance. The great apostle cannot forget the sins of his youth. "I am," he says, "the least of the apostles, who am not worthy to be called an apostle, because I persecuted the Church of God."[18] "A faithful saying and worthy of all acceptation, that Christ Jesus

[14] 1 Pet. 2:13.

[15] 1 Pet. 5:5-8.

[16] 1 Pet. 4:7.

[17] 1 Pet. 2:17.

[18] 1 Cor. 15:9.

came into this world to save sinners, of whom I am the chief. But for this cause have I obtained mercy, that in me first Christ Jesus might show forth all patience, for the information of them that shall believe in Him unto life everlasting."[19]

Penitence deserving the name, then, is not a mere passing act but a permanent state — a supernatural sorrow not fitfully but continually welling up within us, a condition of soul lasting until death. At no stage of the spiritual life may we dispense with it. It is necessary for the one who has advanced in virtue, as well as for the hardened sinner.

We are reminded of this in Confession. When slight imperfections form the subject matter of our accusation, the priest may ask us to recall, in a general way, some former mortal sin, if any, or other venial sins, and to include them in our act of contrition. This is done to enliven our sense of sin and to increase our repentance.

Wondrously retentive is the sinner's memory. The reason is that the remembrance of past guilt and of God's grace, which raised the sinner from spiritual death to supernatural life, can coexist in the soul. God's own

[19] 1 Tim. 1:15, 16.

eternity seems to be stamped upon the sinner's conscience, that he may not be without fear for forgiven sin, that the abiding knowledge of former sin and the punishment thereof may, all his days, wring from him the wail that will finally remove the least vestige of both sin and punishment. "Wash me yet more from my iniquity, and cleanse me from my sin."[20]

As, in the physical order, there is no light without its shadow, so, in the moral order, although the light of grace illumines the soul, the dim reflection of the hated past still remains. The God who assumed our flesh so that sinners might "have life and have it more abundantly,"[21] the God of infinite compassion who came "to seek and to save that which was lost,"[22] would have us ever reflect on our past sinfulness — not to weaken our confidence in His unspeakable mercy and to fill us with despair, but to enliven our sorrow and to strengthen our love of Him, so that "where sin abounded, grace might more abound."[23]

[20] Ps. 50:4 (RSV = Ps. 51:2).

[21] John 10:10.

[22] Luke 19:10.

[23] Cf. Rom. 5:20.

The habitual thought of former sin will invigorate present repentance. "If we say we have no sin, we deceive ourselves, and the truth is not in us."[24] True self-knowledge will beget "the sorrow that is according to God," which "worketh penance steadfast unto salvation."

Thus, the prayer of the publican — "O God, be merciful to me a sinner"[25] — we can never repeat too often; his humility we can never assimilate too well. The yearning to return to the God whom he had outraged, the conscious recognition of his sin, which convinced him that he was utterly unworthy of pardon, justified him fully in the sight of the divine majesty. "I say to you, this man went down into his house justified."[26]

Realizing that we are sinners, we must have a godly, and thus a deep, humble, sincere, perennial, and efficacious sorrow for our sins, a sorrow that forces us to quit the broad, rough road of sin and, with renewed spiritual strength, to advance in the way of God.

If we evade the stern obligation of repentance, we shall be lost. "Unless you shall do penance, you shall all

[24] 1 John 1:8.

[25] Luke 18:13.

[26] Luke 18:14.

likewise perish."[27] Sorrow for past sin is the infallible means of avoiding future sin. Penitence is, then, the rock foundation of a virtuous life. We must clothe ourselves with the penitential garb here, if we would escape the terrors of the judgment hereafter. "If Thou, O Lord, wilt mark iniquities, Lord, who shall stand it?"[28]

[27] Luke 13:3.

[28] Ps. 129:3 (RSV = Ps. 130:3).

Chapter Two

Found your repentance on Christ's tender mercy

"Christ Jesus came into the world to save sinners."

1 Timothy 1:15

There is a singular moral fitness in the manner in which Christ redeemed us. In this stupendous mystery of divine love, it was proper that man should suffer because man had sinned. Man had sinned by disobedience inspired by pride. It was fitting that Christ should atone for man's sin by obedience unto the death of the Cross,[29] and by a humiliation deep enough to reduce Him to the level of a mere "worm and no man; the reproach of men and the outcast of the people."[30] It was eminently proper that Christ should die, because death was the punishment for man's sin.

The amazing love that prompted our redemption, the self-sacrificing love that endured the most agonizing tortures for sinners who, far from having a claim on that love, deserved only eternal chastisement — this appeals

[29] Phil. 2:8.

[30] Ps. 21:7 (RSV = Ps. 22:6).

to our finest sensibilities, stirs most profoundly our natural inclinations, and stimulates most intensely our own affections. No passion moves us more readily and more deeply than love. And when love is gratuitous, wholly disinterested, when we have insulted Him who loves us, and, instead of condemning us forever, He suffers and dies for us, words cannot express our wonderment.

It is "the charity of God . . . poured forth in our hearts by the Holy Spirit who is given to us"[31] that establishes "peace with God, through our Lord Jesus Christ."[32] The death of Christ is the charity of God most impressively manifested. "For scarce for a just man will one die; yet perhaps for a good man someone would dare to die. But God commendeth His charity toward us, because when as yet we were sinners according to the time, Christ died for us."[33]

The love of Christ in His sufferings and death excites to rapturous ecstasy the most sublime of the passions, and man gives himself to God. Hence the great apostle, recounting the reasons for our hope in Christ,

[31] Rom. 5:5.

[32] Rom. 5:1.

[33] Rom. 5:7-9.

joyously exclaims: "If, when we were enemies, we were reconciled to God by the death of His Son, much more, being reconciled, shall we be saved by His life. And not only so, but also we glory in God, through our Lord Jesus Christ, by whom we have now received reconciliation."[34]

In the revelation of a great mystery, it is characteristic of Divine Providence to select as its instrument of communication one whose soul is best suited to receive its truth.

St. Paul, in his conversion, is a striking illustration of this fact. Hurled to earth at the climax of his insanely relentless persecution of the Christians, he is at once changed into a docile servant of God's love;[35] that love elicits a response from the deepest depths of his ardently passionate nature and inspires him with lifelong gratitude to his eternal Benefactor. Henceforth, he becomes the eloquent preacher of the wondrous effects of repentance in the soul of the most hardened sinner through the mercy which God lavished so generously upon man in the mystery of the Redemption.

[34] Rom. 5:10-11.

[35] Acts 9:3-4, 6.

This truth is the substance of his letter. On this theme, his language thrills. His words to the Ephesians on this subject burn with his inspiration: "God, who is rich in mercy, for His exceeding charity wherewith He loved us, even when we were dead in sins, hath quickened us together in Christ, by whose grace you are saved, and hath raised us up together and hath made us sit together in the heavenly places, through Christ Jesus, that He might show in the ages to come the abundant riches of His grace, in His bounty toward us in Christ Jesus."[36]

The realization of the love of Christ in His Passion is as necessary to the life of repentance as the soul is to the life of the body. David, the illustrious penitent of the Old Law, is a notable exponent of this truth. The Passion is the soul of his psalms. His nature, if we are to judge from his repeated allusions to the sufferings of Christ, was made exquisitely sensitive, and thus prepared for the reception of the priceless gift of "a contrite and humble heart";[37] through his habitual meditation on the Redeemer's transcendent love for men, his sins were washed away.

[36] Eph. 2:4-7.

[37] Ps. 50:19 (RSV = Ps. 51:17).

In the New Law, the thief on the cross is the most luminous example of deep, sincere repentance. His keenly searching insight into the eternal meaning of Christ's death, the effect of his correspondence with grace, revealed to him the magnitude of the Savior's love for sinners: it made him a saint.[38]

Another pointed illustration of the love of Christ in His Passion is our Lord's insistent question to St. Peter: "Lovest thou me?"[39] Christ aimed to make his penitence perennial by arousing in him an intensely ardent reciprocal love for the Master, whose love in the supreme sacrifice had first inspired the sorrow that suffused His apostle's soul.

Once the perception of Christ's love is awakened, it must deepen. And the more it deepens, the greater will be our detestation of sin, which caused the Savior's terrible giving of Himself for sinners. As our hatred of sin increases, so much the greater will be our progress in true repentance. Penitence, therefore, flows from our appreciation of Christ's love for us in His sufferings, and consequently the strength of our repentance must be

[38] Luke 23:40-43.

[39] John 21:16.

measured by the keenness of our appreciation of that love.

Reflection upon the Passion cannot but excite in our souls "the sorrow that is according to God."[40] The malice of sin is best studied in the school of the Cross. Sin humiliated Christ beyond human comprehension. In taking flesh, the eternal God "emptied Himself."[41] But, were it not for our sins, pain and sorrow might never have touched Him as man. The majesty of the Godhead might, in all its eternal splendor, have shone through the entrancing beauty of the perfect manhood.

The life of Christ on earth might have been painless. But what a change man's sin wrought in the Redeemer! The mental anguish within, the physical torture without, the withering sorrow, the solitary loneliness, the long, sharp thorns driven into the skull, the bones laid bare by the steel whips, the wasted form covered with gashes, crimsoned with blood, the hands and feet pierced with nails — what a heartrending figure, what a "Man of Sorrows"[42] our sins made of Christ! The light and the

[40] 2 Cor. 7:10.

[41] Phil. 2:7.

[42] Isa. 53:3.

peace, the joy and the rest, that might have been His as He walked with men, were turned into darkness, pain, and agonizing death.

As often as we sin grievously, we "crucify again to ourselves the Son of God and make Him a mockery."[43] Externally, our sins cannot affect Christ, cannot nail Him to the Cross; but internally, He can still experience the sinner's malice, his treachery, his ingratitude. The sinner can still wound the Heart that has loved man so much, can still cry out: "Crucify Him! Crucify Him!"[44]

Man can, by mortal sin, also frustrate the effect of Christ's Passion and death. He can void the life of grace and all its consequences, which the Savior bought for us so dearly. The direct results of the soul's correspondence with grace are the thrilling joy and the yearning for spiritual progress, which seize the soul in the eternal embrace of divine love and make it the habitation of its God, for "if anyone love me, he will keep my word, and my Father will love him, and we will come to him and make our abode with him."[45] Also a result of the soul's

[43] Cf. Heb. 6:6.

[44] Luke 23:21; John 19:6.

[45] John 14:23.

correspondence with grace is the life of grace itself, which adorns the soul with ravishing beauty in virtue of its most intimate union with God. All this, sin blights, crushes, and stills. Sin in its deadly evil is the great enemy of the Cross of Christ, opposing the designs of His eternal pity, robbing the soul of the fruit of His sufferings, and trampling underfoot His Precious Blood.

In every true penitent, as the realization of these effects deepens, the appreciation of divine forgiveness intensifies. And as the appreciation of divine forgiveness intensifies, repentance, man's real life, develops, impelling him to forsake sin and to imitate more closely Him who delivered Himself for sinners.

The abiding consciousness of God's love manifested in His constant act of forgiveness is the measure of the growth of the life of true penitence. How often, in the sacrament of mercy and reconciliation, does Christ's mercy embrace our souls! How often does the Precious Blood flow from the Savior's Heart, that source of perpetual pardon, into the soul of the sinner, washing away his sins and imparting to him a peaceful newness of life through the revival in him of the effects of the Passion!

Each sacramental absolution is an act of love emanating from the divine Heart, throbbing with love for sinners. In the Lord's Prayer, we are taught to have daily recourse to this eternal forgiving love. As the waves of the ocean follow one another in ceaseless succession to break, one at a time, on the shore, so the Savior's love ever pleads before the throne of mercy, and we experience God's continual forgiveness separately each time it calms our troubled souls by remitting, in the fullness of its compassion, all their guilt, and restoring their supernatural life. Not the fact of forgiveness or our need of it, but the realization of the reiterated act of forgiveness is the principle of the growth of the true penitential spirit.

Tenderness, moreover, which is the striking feature of repentance, develops from a consciousness of this unceasing pardon. Bodily chastisements, although great in their power to sanctify us, make for austerity of character and often minister to our vanity and self-sufficiency. But sorrow for sin born of Christ's eternal mercy to sinners renders us intensely and perpetually penitent, invigorates our souls with divine energy, quickens in us the sense of our total dependence upon God, and thus strengthens our devotion by establishing it on the rock of humility.

It is therefore a mighty defense against temptation, for sorrow for past sin inspires in us a salutary fear, and hence safeguards us against the commission of future sin. We can best imitate that tender compassion of Christ, which springs from His sorrow over the enormity of sin, by deepening our appreciation of the evil of our transgressions and of the greatness of God's love evinced by His merciful forgiveness of them.

As we grow in this beautiful, expressive tenderness, we become more patient with our neighbor's weakness, more sympathetic with him in his struggle for righteousness, and more merciful to him when he sins.

And oh, how urgently we need to learn this lesson! We are, after God has forgiven us, prone to plume ourselves upon our restored powers as if we were absolutely sure of never sinning again, and to frown upon and condemn our fellowman who is still the victim of sin. We may wish even to usurp God's place and to subject our neighbor to what we unjustly label our "just indignation," by expressing to him, perhaps very unkindly and very crudely, our censorious judgment of his conduct, falsely reasoning that our caustic appraisal of the sinner redounds to the greater glory of God.

Our own freedom from sin is often the measure of our intolerance of a brother sinner. The higher our exaltation by grace, the more liable we are to be niggardly in sympathy for the fallen. When we need mercy, we are willingly merciful. The realization of our own shortcomings may beget forbearance with the faults of others. Sinners are very broad in their interpretation of sin. But when we leave the crooked highway of sin and proceed along the straight path of virtue, then should we enlarge our sympathy for the weaknesses of others; the more we pity them, and the kinder and the gentler we are with their infirmities, the more we develop our own penitence.

We can best learn to know and to develop compassion for others by daily meditation on the Passion. Our appreciation of the love that moved Christ toward us is the touchstone of the growth of our compassion toward others.

Forbearance with the imperfect must not, of course, diminish our sorrow for their weakness. Largeness of sympathy for the sinner does not mean a palliation of his sins. Nevertheless, we sorely need to cultivate the spirit of considerateness for the sinner. We fulfill the law of God by mutual forbearance. "Bear ye one another's burdens, and so you shall fulfill the law of Christ."[46]

[46] Gal. 6:2.

We cannot imitate Christ unless we are led by His spirit. His mercy did not censure but embraced our sin-stained souls and snatched them from eternal ruin. And even after having forgiven us, He does not upbraid us, but is infinitely patient with us, throwing the mantle of His love over our innumerable sins, ever pleading with His eternal Father for us, and drawing us by His marvelously magnetic mercy to surrender ourselves wholly to Him who "emptied Himself" for us.

O Infinite Lover of men, warm our cold hearts
with the fire of Thy divine love.
Thou, O God, art love, and Thou hast said:
"By this shall all men know that you are my disciples:
if you have love one for another."
Give us the fullness of Thy spirit of forbearance
in dealing with our fellowman, and touch us with
the tenderness of Thy gentle forgiveness of his faults
so that, loving him for Thy sake,
we may abide in Thy love here
and reign eternally with Thee hereafter.

What a power is this forgiving love! The more we feel its mature effects, the more we yearn to impart it to others. Diffusive by nature, it spreads from soul to soul, binding them together in a community of Christlike forgetfulness of the past, inspiring them with hope for the future, and perfecting their love of God through the consciousness of a more intimate union with Him. When this spirit of repentance is rich, full, and free, we become the elect of God and realize more fully that all men are brothers, and that therefore the need of our neighbor is the same as our own.

Thus St. Paul says: "Put ye on therefore, as the elect of God, holy and beloved . . . mercy, benignity, humility, modesty, patience; bearing with one another, and forgiving one another, if any have a complaint against another. Even as the Lord hath forgiven you, so do you also. But above all these things, have charity, which is the bond of perfection."[47] The great apostle states the infallible effect of such conduct: "And let the peace of Christ rejoice in your hearts, wherein also you are called in one body."[48]

Thus we become co-laborers with Christ, humble instruments in His hands, His representatives in bringing into the souls of our brethren the eternal results of

[47] Col. 3:12-14.

[48] Col. 3:15.

the Redemption; renewing, by our spirit of forgiveness and forbearance, the love of God in their hearts, and enlivening our own hope of salvation by energizing them with the confidence that must finally issue in endless joy: "For if, when we were enemies, we were reconciled to God by the death of His Son; much more, being reconciled, shall we be saved by His life."

Chapter Three

Let sorrow for sin help you overcome your sins

"For I know my iniquity,
and my sin is always before me."

Psalm 50:5
(RSV = Psalm 51:3)

The more accurately we appraise God's sanctity and the consequent completeness of His condemnation of evil, the more deeply shall we know the malice of sin, and hence, the more sincerely and enduringly shall we repent. But true repentance forces its way down to the soul's profoundest consciousness very slowly. In the hardened sinner especially, the moral sense is only gradually quickened to anxious sensitiveness over the commission of his sin.

What uncertainty, what vacillation, what irresolution, what doubt, what dimness of vision, what partial hopes, what slow, fitful enlightenment, what conflicting struggles attend such a soul's effort to rid itself of sin! God's mercy works to free the soul from its slavery, and sin ever strives to keep it within the narrow confines of its deceitful captivity; God's grace ever seeks to illumine it, and the darkness of sin ever deepens, to blind its eyes; the soul yearns to be released from its merciless thralldom, yet is so attached to sin, so mired in sin, as to fear that God will not release it. But grace by degrees refines the soul's moral sense, clarifies gradually its vision, until it beholds, to the full extent of its limited powers, the hideousness of sin and God's ineffable mercy; and smiting the soul, as it did St. Paul, with the consciousness of its desolation, grace finally snaps asunder the chains of its degrading slavery.

What an experience was the sense of our first sin! Perhaps our dormant powers were awakened to the consideration of our diseased state by a sermon, by the death of a dear friend, by "the dread of something after death, the undiscovered country from whose bourne no traveler returns,"[49] by a sudden illumination of grace piercing the darkness, and causing the scales to fall from our souls' eyes.[50]

But what a change was effected in our spiritual lives! Even souls schooled in the art of self-discipline, insistently "mortifying by the Spirit the deeds of the flesh,"[51]

[49] William Shakespeare, *Hamlet*, Act 3, scene 1, line 56.

[50] Cf. Acts 9:18.

[51] Cf. Rom. 8:13.

daily subjecting the natural to the supernatural, have experienced this ever-memorable smiting of their spiritual sensibilities over the commission of sin.

How lasting and how profitable is the undying remembrance of such a crisis! How eventful the change wrought by it in the soul's life! What a complete conversion it worked in the soul of the slave of sin, deciding for him, perhaps, his eternal salvation! What a renewal of fervor, what a stimulus to progress in virtue, now seizes the regenerated soul!

The crisis has instilled the spirit of self-reproach, which, in its sincerity — beholding the soul's sinfulness, and realizing that there is much more to be repented of and that to bring to light hidden sins is a positive sign of growth in holiness — broadens and deepens the penitential spirit. The soul now realizes that its past sorrow has been without the depth that would enable it to atone for its sins, and it loves God all the more from the conviction born of the knowledge of the guilt of these lapses, and God's infinite patience with them. And as the soul's love of Him becomes purer from the consciousness of its guilt, so likewise does its repentance ever increase.

The touchstone of remorse is sorrow of soul inspired by the conviction of sin. It is a sorrow which beholds sin with a vivid and unchanging appreciation of its malice, which constantly contemplates the pain and anguish that sin caused the Redeemer, which gazes with fixed vision on the eternal consequences of sin. This indispensable prerequisite of the true penitential spirit is ever active in the soul to deepen its detestation and sharpen its vision by associating it more closely with Christ's vision of sin, thereby increasing the soul's hatred of the guilt of sin; this hatred of sin grows with advancing years and becomes perfect only when the soul enters God's eternal court, where sorrow shall be no more.

Godly sorrow aroused by the power of grace working remorse in the soul may be transient or permanent. When the conscience of the sinner is first smitten with the sense of sin, he is impulsive, restless, morose, yearns for self-denial, and almost blinds himself to the mercy of God through a false idea of His justice. This unreasonable sorrow soon passes, under the powerful stimulus of grace, into sorrow that is reasonable and permanent. The soul foregoes its violence and grows calm; its fear of God is no longer slavish, but reverential; it becomes more patient with, although not indulgent of, itself; its grief is now silent rather than assertive, because it has penetrated beneath the surface.

Secure in the possession of Him who cannot change, the soul is not eager for fitful sensible fervor. Grounded in humility, it is more vigilant, but also not dejected when it falls. Wholly diffident of itself, it clothes itself with the very strength of God by its childlike trust in Him. Sorrow springing from remorse may, in its twofold aspect, be likened to a river swelling and overflowing its banks, sweeping all before it in its fury, but by degrees subsiding as it sinks into the absorbent soil.

But permanent sorrow has its stages. Even in its advanced state, there is often a trace of the force and assertiveness of its first manifestation. As the soul becomes more keenly receptive to grace, its sense of sin grows, and bitter sorrow makes itself felt at the sight of even slight faults, as it formerly was convulsed by poignant grief for serious sins. The soul's consciousness of sin has been so quickened, its vision is now so sharp, its appreciation of the sanctity of God and the severity of His justice is now so true, that it is transfixed with fear at the least violation of His law.

In the warmth of growing faith, habitual, quieter, and deeper sorrow gradually gains the ascendancy, and, slowly but surely, it leads the soul to the heights of holiness.

To suppose that sorrow does not exist because it is not demonstrative is a fallacy. Sorrow is very much akin to love. In its first fervor, love is vehement, yearns to express itself, is urgent to prove its sincerity. When it grows calm and wholly possesses the soul, becoming an unfailing source of kindness, self-sacrifice, and inviolable fidelity to duty, love is then the soul's sublimest passion. At first, it was only a fleeting emotion; now it is a fixed state following the dictates of reason, and thus befitting an intelligent creature. Likewise, sorrow for sin, which divests repentance of excitability and makes it conform to the stern law of duty, far from languishing, acquires a more secure hold on the principles of the higher life.

The striving of the soul to rid itself of sin is the best evidence of the progress of its remorse. We are more certain of our sin than of our penitence. We know our sin directly; only by inference from its practical results can we prove our penitence. Only when the conviction of our sin is so rooted that it touches with healing the very source of our sin — only then are we sincerely repentant.

The sinner, however, no matter how depraved, does not love sin for its own sake. As the intellect clings to error, not because of the error, but because it beholds at least a modicum of truth in it, so the will consents to evil because it appears good. We are enamored, not of sin in itself, but only of the effects of sin. The man who circumvents his neighbor loves, not the trickery involved in deception so diabolical, but the result of it, the gain that he thinks will accrue to him. The acquisition of wealth is very powerful in its appeal to the man who is sordidly materialistic, but the duplicity and dishonesty that he may resort to in amassing a fortune cannot but be distasteful to him.

In short, man may long to gratify his passions, but not for the sake of the sin implicated with such indulgence. The desire to please self is so strong in him that it may stifle all his revulsion to sin and plunge his soul headlong into it. He is attracted by the pleasure the sin gives him; he loves the fountainhead and source of the sin. The satisfaction of his passions urges him on, driving him to trample on grace and its fruit, the desire to please God, which is entirely inconsistent with self-gratification.

Not the malice of sin in itself, but rather, the love of self-indulgence, is the reason for sin. The hatred of sin in itself is not therefore the essential difference between true and false repentance.

True repentance is easily discerned. Mortification is its soul. When we repeatedly resist our ruling passion, when we remove the causes that stir it into action, when we lay the axe to the root of sin, when we are proof against the alluring voice of self-love, which ever seeks to discredit the claims of conscience, when we bridle the triple concupiscence of the world, the flesh, and the Devil, when we are guided by the divine philosophy of the gospel and not by the uncertain, shifting maxims of the world, when the spirit of self-denial has so thoroughly woven itself into the fibers of our religious life as to make us impervious to the poisonous exhalations of worldliness, sensuality, and pride, when there is a substantial, not an accidental change in our attitude toward sin in its complex guises, when the Cross is for us the test and measure of success, when we learn the secret of sanctity from its greatest exponent and exemplar, Jesus Christ, who "did not please Himself,"[52] when we "rend our hearts and not our garments,"[53] and turn wholly to the Lord, our God — then and then only are we truly penitent.

[52] Rom. 15:3.

[53] Cf. Joel 2:13.

The soul sincerely repentant appreciates the force of Christ's words: "Watch, and pray that you enter not into temptation. The spirit indeed is willing, but the flesh is weak."[54] Such a soul is ever watchful, keenly conscious of the many subtle distempers of the human heart, ever ready to fight courageously against the passions that may, in an instant, be kindled into a mighty conflagration within it, ever on its guard lest the enemy surprise it openly or lead it covertly into the occasions of sin, deepening its confidence in God by increasingly distrusting its own strength. On the contrary, the soul that is not truly penitent still hankers after the seductive sweetness of sin; it flees not its devious paths; its enchanting spell still lulls the soul to sleep; self-love, and not the love of God, still rules supreme.

With such a soul, amendment is not a firm, efficacious resolve, but a mere weak wish that is powerless to withstand the stress and storm of temptation. The soul in this state, without the abiding conviction of sin, cannot renounce itself nor arouse the spirit of self-denial so essential to sincere repentance. The supreme need of such a soul is a strong sense of the sanctity of God, and

[54] Mark 14:38.

of His consequent detestation of sin as revealed in the punishment which He reserves for it hereafter.

The essential difference between true and false repentance shows the indisputable necessity of sincerity with God. Our service of God must be free from duplicity. Christ enforces this truth: "He that is not with me is against me."[55] God cannot tolerate any compromise with sin: "He that gathereth not with me scattereth."[56] The man who tries to bargain with God is a weakling. To confess and not to change is treason against God. The eye of the soul must be sound. To the conviction that we are sinners, we must add honesty in dealing with our sins and in addressing ourselves to God for their pardon. Grace not only can reveal to the soul its characteristic weakness — without the cloak in which dishonest self-love would hide it — but also can counteract the deadly poison of sin and give the soul the moral strength to overcome the treacherous tempter.

Just as the vividness of the sense of sin is the measure of the growth of penitence, repentance is the great law of spiritual progress for both saint and sinner. But

[55] Matt. 12:30.

[56] Ibid.

paradoxical as it may seem, the penitential spirit is more fully developed in the saint than in the sinner. The saint's foundation of holiness is laid, and its superstructure mounts higher through watchfulness, prayer, and fasting. These are the means he uses to prevent carnal darkness from curtaining the eyes of his soul. He is convinced that he bears in his flesh the seeds of sin. He realizes that he carries about with him a body prone to sin.

Constantly reflecting upon the records of human corruption in the world about him, he beholds with the power of ever-broadening vision the sources of sin within him. He knows that his heart is a miniature of the great heart of humanity, and the melancholy monuments along the high road of history which he daily beholds are cautionary signals warning him against the snares that threaten his own spiritual ruin. Conscious that he is a child of sin, he checks his vicious tendencies and restrains his passions by drastic self-discipline.

Such penitence is essentially progressive. As the soul quits the haunts of sin and grows in virtue, its sorrow for sin must increase because, under the searching rays of truth that enlighten the soul as it tries to reach a higher plane of moral rectitude, it sees the essential difference between the oppressive darkness of its former sinful state and the pure, invigorating atmosphere of sanctity which it now breathes, and it better appreciates the miracle of mercy performed by God in working so marked a change in it. The soul inured to a life of repentance, ever maintaining its empire over the infirmities of the flesh, will utter its act of deepest, most godly sorrow at the hour of death. As long, however, as the soul lingers in its prison, regardless of its advances in sanctity, persevering penitence is absolutely necessary.

"Blessed is the man that feareth the Lord."[57] "Converse in fear during the time of your sojourning here."[58] "With fear and trembling work out your salvation."[59] "He that thinketh himself to stand, let him take heed lest he fall."[60]

These words are addressed to both saint and sinner. The fear of the Lord, the crown of all the gifts of the Holy Spirit,[61] is an essential part of the penitential spirit.

[57] Ps. 111:1 (RSV = Ps. 112:1).

[58] 1 Pet. 1:17.

[59] Phil. 2:12.

[60] 1 Cor. 10:12.

[61] The seven gifts of the Holy Spirit are knowledge, wisdom, understanding, counsel, fortitude, piety, and fear of the Lord; see Isa. 11:2.

Christ our model availed Himself of this gift, "who in the days of His flesh, with a strong cry and tears, offering up prayers and supplications to Him who was able to save Him from death, was heard for His reverence."[62]

The possibility that we may lose our souls is a thought well calculated to strike terror into our hearts. Fear must therefore be the sustaining nourishment of our sorrow. If we fear God, He will hear our sighs, and we will swiftly proceed along the rugged but royal way of repentance until we arrive at the mountain of God.

Habitual penitence is the infallible test of growth in holiness, of the depth of its penetration, and the sincerity and consistency of its profession. The spirit of self-condemnation and of profound abasement must be the food ever feeding the energies of our resistance and self-denial, renewing our powers of self-discipline, restraining our tendency to indulgence, which is born of self-love, and strengthening us in the hour of trial by tightening our hold on God.

In the light of these truths, Lent, the season of serious thought and solemn penitence, should exert a dominant influence upon the soul aspiring to closer union

[62] Heb. 5:7.

with God. During this sacred time, the Church bids her children to scrutinize with care the plain, bare, searching truths of her sublime moral code. Somber in penitential garb, she invites them to contemplate the "Man of Sorrows"[63] and to lay the deep foundation of veritable repentance by meditation on what it cost Him to redeem us.

The voice of God, during these forty days, seems to speak more clearly, perhaps because the ears of our souls are more sensitively attuned by grace to catch its faintest whisper. It gently chides us and thus awakens within us the power of remorse. It strengthens our conviction that we are sinners and, opening the sluices of our sorrow when we confess, wafts the wail of our heartfelt grief to the throne of God. We hear the echo of God's forgiveness in the words of absolution; and the smile of God, appeased again, illumines our souls. Whether smiting us directly or sharply reproving us through its divinely appointed oracles, it is the voice of love.

What more singular proof of God's mercy to sinners than His perennial pursuit of their souls? Now He speaks to them sternly through mental anguish or bodily pain;

[63] Isa. 53:3.

at another time, He humiliates them to the dust by the loss of earthly possessions or the coldness of ardently cherished friends. Thus He rouses them from their spiritual inertia to the serious consideration of the ravages of sin within them and the danger of eternal loss; and so, inspirited with the fear of the Lord and made "wise unto sobriety,"[64] they forsake sin and adorn their souls with the virtues that will render them precious in His sight and be the pledge of their eternal union with Him.

[64] Rom. 12:3.

Chapter Four

Combat your pride through sacramental Confession

"Receive ye the Holy Spirit.
Whose sins you shall forgive,
they are forgiven them:
and whose sins you shall retain,
they are retained."

John 20:22, 23

Confession is the quickening element of the soul's restoration to the friendship of God. It is consequently an essential feature of true, practical repentance.

Humiliating as it is, the sinner should remember that the best antidote for counteracting the pride necessarily associated with the commission of any sin is the abasement entailed by Confession.

And the sinner is not alone in experiencing this humiliation; he shares it with Christ. The Redeemer bore not only the punishment of sin, but also its debasing shame. Nothing can be more touching than this revelation of Christ's love for His fallen creatures; the mystery of His humiliation is not merely the veiling under human form of the ineffable, eternal splendor of the Godhead, but His assumption of the weakness of frail, dependent mortals. Christ became a penitent for man, bearing the weight of man's sins as if they were His own.

In His circumcision, Christ put on the livery of sinners. By submitting to this act, which was the distinctive mark of sinners, He signed Himself with the sign of their condemnation, thus becoming for them an outcast among His brethren through His free acceptance of the burden of common humanity. How profound the humiliation of this act of self-denial for souls — Christ branding Himself with the mark of sinners, assuming their sins as if they were His own! The humility shown by this act deepened steadily throughout the various heartrending scenes of the Savior's martyrdom until He "emptied Himself"[65] on Calvary.

As the bud contains the rose, so the fuller revelations of the life of God incarnate are latent in their less striking manifestations. His three days' loss and His being found by Mary and Joseph[66] symbolized the sorrow of the separation following His death and burial, and the joy of His glorious Resurrection. The momentary glimpse of His divinity that the chosen three beheld on Tabor[67] was anticipatory of the fuller, permanent glory with which

[65] Phil. 2:7.

[66] Luke 2:43-46.

[67] Matt. 17:1-2; Mark 9:1-2; Luke 9:28-29.

He would finally adorn His human nature. So likewise, when He freely became a penitent for sinners, there were crises in His humiliating avowal of sin, the thought of which should make us mute with wonderment.

In His agony, as the vengeance of the Father fell upon Him, He felt in His deepest soul the weight of the accumulated sins of mankind, freely accepting them, lovingly acknowledging Himself their bearer as if He were guilty of them all.

While Christ's agony — when the full pressure of the concentrated iniquities of a doomed race sank into His sorely afflicted soul — was an act in which the avowal of the sins He accepted as His own was distinctly stressed, He anticipated during His life this one signal penitential immolation of Himself. He appeared among those who, under the powerful stimulus of grace, sought baptism of the virile precursor, John the Baptist. That the hope of a fallen race might not perish forever, the curse of the sins of humanity must fall on Him, and He must acknowledge before the world His free acceptance thereof. By His baptism, Christ voluntarily took the place of the sinner, so that He might, through the assumption of the sinner's shame, wipe out his sin and reconcile him to his God.

When we repent, Christ's acknowledgment of sin thus establishes a bond of union between Him and us. It is not that His acceptance of our burden releases us from the obligation of doing penance, or frees us from the confession of our guilt. In this, as in every other detail of His life, He is our model. Apart from His words, which make Confession a positive duty, His acknowledgment of our sin is a strong incentive to us to practice it. When we confess, we are not spared the shame and confusion of this hard task, but our sins are greatly diminished by the thought that we share in His humiliation, and consequently render ourselves most dear to Him; for "a contrite and humbled heart, O God, Thou wilt not despise."[68]

The God-Man is the source of all grace to souls. Through His death, He has reconciled us to the Father, who "loveth the Son and showeth Him all things which He doth . . . and He hath given Him power to do judgment, because He is the Son of Man."[69] To seal and to perpetuate His love, He has sent His priests to be the visible channels through which His graces are to flow;

[68] Ps. 50:19 (RSV = Ps. 51:17).

[69] John 5:20, 27.

He has charged them to judge the guilt of their fellowmen and to absolve their sins even as He, the great High Priest, did. Like those to whom they are sent, straitened by the same infirmities, they can have compassion on sinners.

The love of Christ for sinners, and His sympathy with them, vested in the confessor, are very powerful as an inducement to the penitent to submit to the act of self-abasement involved in the telling of his sins. The realization of the eternal results of a good confession is of itself sufficient to enable even the most hardened sinner to undergo the momentary embarrassment of unburdening himself to the confessor. The sinner must judge himself now, so that he may escape the terrors of his final judgment before the assembled world. "If we would judge ourselves, we should not be judged. But whilst we are judged, we are chastised by the Lord, that we be not condemned with this world."[70] The sincerity and humility of the secret manifestation of our sins to the confessor will forestall their public exposure at the last judgment. Christ will hide our guilt from the eyes of the world if we now, with deep sorrow for our sins, tear

[70] 1 Cor. 11:31-32.

asunder the veil of self-love that would hide them from His representative.

As the thought of the Last Judgment presents itself in full force to our minds, we should subject our consciences to the anticipative equivalent of the singular strictness and searching severity of our examination before the whole world. The moral law within us echoes God's law above us.

Truth, then, should be the soul of the scrutiny we direct to the deepest secrets of our hearts. Our examination and confession must reflect, as far as possible, the justice and unsparingness of our final exposure before our fellowmen. We must sift our consciences honestly and impartially. We must rid ourselves of the spirit of compromise that often conceals vice by the specious pretext of necessity and whittles away guilt by all kinds of subtle sophistry. The miasmic exhalations of our pride must not blind the eyes of our souls.

We must look sin squarely in the face, and not seek, with self-gratifying reasons, to disguise the guilt of its commission. Although we must weigh doubts without scrupulosity, we must not always decide them in our favor. Our examination must embrace every serious infraction of God's law in thought, word, and deed. Nor are we to exclude our free cooperation in the grave sins of others. Sins of omission as well as sins of commission must likewise enter into the examination of our guilt. In a word, we must judge ourselves justly here, if we hope to escape the visitation of Christ's eternal justice hereafter.

The mature moral result of Confession is its humiliation. If God commanded us to confess to Him alone, our sorrow would perhaps be as deep, and our purpose of amendment as sincere, but it would not be as humiliating as the truthful disclosure of our sins to a fellowman. We are so constituted by nature that the visible affects us more than the invisible. Very little humiliation would therefore accompany the secret telling of our sins, just as, indeed, very little shame and embarrassment accompany their commission before the veiled face of the unseen yet ever-present God.

The fruitful confusion associated with Confession, which often prevents recourse to it, is an inestimable benefit. It overthrows our pride, the cause of all our sins; it deepens our humility, the foundation of all virtue, by making us share in Christ's unspeakable humiliations; it confounds us before one instead of millions.

Furthermore, from another angle, Confession is especially beneficial. A thought expressed is a far more palpable reality than when it remains a mere mental existence. Words clarify the vagueness of ideas. They imprint themselves upon the mind with a vividness wholly beyond the power of what is unformulated. Words can fill the heart with joy or crush it with sorrow, whereas thoughts not shaped in words, and therefore dormant, can wield no such influence.

How often does even the most obstinate sinner wince at the mere mention of the word that names the sensuality that degrades him to the level of the brute, that describes the hypocrisy that brands him with the duplicity of Hell! The expression of the sin in words is a living power that often swiftly changes the course of a life. The spoken word has a substantial form, and hence a permanence not possessed by the bodiless, fleeting thought. It is a finger of scorn that points unerringly at the sinner's crime, and thus increases the consciousness of his guilt.

Remarkable, then, as a means of developing our repentance is the moral result of Confession. Self-delusion alone can defeat this salutary effect. Even the devout are often victims of this fatal vice. If Confession falls under the baneful influence of moral cowardice, if it is the mask of our duplicity, if it hides our hypocrisy, the iron hand of the father of lies has seized our souls and we are hurrying to Hell over the broad road of final impenitence. We must therefore be on our guard lest our confession itself need repentance. We must beware lest the humiliation of the acknowledgment of our sins feed our pride. We must not deceive ourselves by the persuasion that repentance ends with the forgiveness of our sins, and thus freely expose ourselves and fall an easy prey to the same occasions of sin.

As we are creatures of habit, we must exercise special care when we confess frequently. Change being the law of our existence, constant repetition dulls the appreciation of what we do. An act often repeated is apt to become very commonplace.

Not merely the relief of a burdened conscience, which continually urges, under the influence of grace, the habitual sinner to confess, after years of sin, but progress in virtue — this should be the absorbing idea of frequent confessions. Frequent confessions should be the means of sharpening our spiritual vision to see the malice of sin, and thus of inspiring us with a greater hatred of sin. From keen insight into sin, a yearning to advance in holiness should be a habit of our souls, even though we still suffer the obdurate assaults of the wily tempter.

What peace of mind follows the humble, sincere acknowledgment of our sins! What comfort the soul experiences that, with childlike simplicity and intense penitential love of Christ, unburdens itself of its vices, sinking down beneath the Cross with "the sorrow that is according to God!"[71] What joy thrills the penitent after the confessor has pronounced the wondrous words of redeeming love and creative power: "I absolve you" — words that touch and open the springs of Christ's compassion and forgiveness!

How free and full is the Savior's mercy to sinners! If we but turn to Him with sorrow and confess our sins, He will turn to us and His mercy will, with undying solicitude, embrace our souls. "Why will you die, O house of Israel? 'Turn to me,' saith the Lord of hosts, 'and I will turn to you.' "[72]

[71] 2 Cor. 7:10.

[72] Ezek. 33:11; Zech. 1:3.

Chapter Five

Make reparation for your sins

"As you have yielded your members
to serve uncleanness and iniquity,
unto iniquity, so now yield your members
to serve justice, unto sanctification."

Romans 6:19

Comprehensive in its content, true repentance embraces confession, satisfaction, and amendment. Our sorrow will be "the sorrow that is according to God," producing a repentance which leads to salvation, if, united with Christ, we learn the significant lesson of self-immolation inspired by the same spirit that led Him to offer Himself as a victim for our sins.

We instinctively feel that, for the injury done by sin, we must, as far as possible, make full reparation to the God whom we have offended. This instinct assumes the form of a deep sense of gratitude, manifested by a blending of distrust of self, antipathy for the sin committed, unspeakable happiness at being the object of forgiveness so merciful, and an intense yearning to repay our outraged God with loving service, even if the price be life itself.

This instinct, a law of the natural and supernatural life, is satisfaction, the soul of which is self-denial, issuing from the constant longing to placate where sin has abounded. Without amendment, salvation is impossible. Salvation is born of that love without which devotion and gratitude cannot exist. Amendment and improvement are the same, whereas satisfaction is the offering of the soul's spiritually renewed powers and their complete dedication to God. This self-oblation expands and develops with the growth of penitence, and, under the influence of its advancement, nobler impulses and sublimer spiritual ideas seize the soul.

Christ acknowledged, as if He were the culprit, man's sin. This mysterious union between Christ and the sinner, so eloquently expressed in Christ's circumcision, His Baptism, and His agony, also exists in the life of self-oblation of every true penitent. The agony of Christ over sin ended with His death. The sinner's death to self, his life of self-oblation, follows his admission and his realization of this sin.

Christ compensated fully for man's sin. The subtle tempter, "a murderer from the beginning, a liar and the father of lies,"[73] awakened in man's soul astounding pride, higher than the heavens. "You shall be as gods,"

[73] Cf. John 8:44.

said the serpent.[74] But how full the reparation, how perfect the satisfaction the Savior offered for His disloyal creatures! "God from God . . . begotten, not made, one in Being with the Father. Through Him all things were made," the Nicene Creed declares. Christ "emptied Himself, taking the form of a servant."[75] Man had sought equality with the Most High, and God, to atone for the pride of man, descended so low that He called Himself, by the mouth of the psalmist, "a worm and no man: the reproach of men and the outcast of the people."[76]

Through the pride that caused his disobedience, man severed his allegiance to God. The sovereign Lord, coequal with the Father, humbled Himself to the dust, becoming lovingly submissive "even to the death of the Cross."[77] Man willed to be absolutely self-sufficient, and God, to compensate for His creature's gross insubordination, was "mocked and scourged and spat upon"; He "endured the Cross, despising its shame."[78]

[74] Gen. 3:5.

[75] Phil. 2:7.

[76] Ps. 21:7 (RSV = Ps. 22:6).

[77] Phil. 2:8.

[78] Luke 18:32; Heb. 12:2.

The necessary sequel of man's pride and disobedience was his self-indulgence. Man wills to make himself his only master; he wills to follow the tendencies of nature; he wills to extinguish the light of God in his soul.

To satisfy for man's yielding to sinful pleasure, the divine Son became "a man of sorrows and acquainted with infirmity . . . a leper, and as one struck by God and afflicted."[79] He was "led as a sheep to the slaughter," was "dumb as a lamb before his shearer and . . . cut off out of the land of the living."[80] How criminal was man's craven carnality, how perfect Christ's atonement through His sublime self-denial!

Throughout the silent suffering of the God-Man, it was not His agony, scourging, crowning with thorns, and Crucifixion that rendered His sacrifice acceptable to the Father. It was His internal, voluntary self-oblation that gave all, even life itself, restoring to God whole-souled devotion and perfect love. Obedience was the grand characteristic of Christ's labor, patience, anguish, and desolation, which ascended like incense to the Father from the sacrificial altar of the Lamb of God.

[79] Isa. 53:3, 4.

[80] Isa. 53:7, 8.

The satisfaction was complete. Christ, through His perfect holocaust, more than compensated the Father for the glory of which man had robbed Him by sin. The Redeemer's words — "I have a baptism wherewith I am to be baptized. And how am I straitened until it be accomplished!"[81] — reveal the intensity of the yearning to repair the injury done by sin that seizes the soul of the repentant sinner.

This identity of disposition between Christ and the penitent is likewise expressed by the psalmist, who exclaims in the person of Christ, "Sacrifice and offering Thou dost not desire; but Thou hast given me an open ear. Burnt offering and sin offering Thou hast not required. Then said I, 'Lo, I come; in the roll of the book, it is written of me; I delight to do Thy will, O my God; Thy law is within my heart.' "[82] Only Christ, in man's nature, by perfect obedience, could fully atone for man's sin.

But the sufferings of Christ do not dispense with the need for ours, just as His assumption of our sins does not supersede our acknowledgment of them. The example

[81] Luke 12:50.

[82] Ps. 40:6-8 (RSV).

of our Lord is universally applicable. We are morally bound to imitate Him and to be associated most intimately with every phase of His life. There must therefore be identity between His offering and ours. The Savior's satisfaction enhances the dignity of our oblation and renders it acceptable to the Father, but it in no way substitutes for it.

St. Paul teaches this truth very explicitly: "When He said above, 'Thou hast neither desired nor taken pleasure in sacrifices and offerings and burnt offerings and sin offerings' (these are offered according to the law), then He added, 'Lo, I have come to do Thy will.' He abolishes the first in order to establish the second. And by that will, we have been sanctified through the offering of the body of Jesus Christ once for all."[83]

There must, then, be a union between Christ and the penitent through a communion of oblation. Our sacrifices are neither dispensed with nor nullified, but are transformed, sanctified, and rendered acceptable in the sight of God through His infinite sacrifice. It matters not what shape our satisfaction assumes. The peculiar form of suffering, the extent of self-denial, and the

[83] Heb. 10:8-10 (RSV).

particular phase of penitence will vary according to the individual character. But just as man is one, although composed of body and soul, so, too, the spirit animating repentance, however diversely expressed, is and can be essentially one. And the strength of our penitence will be the measure of our appraisal of the glory of God, and of the necessity of full conformity to His will.

Various are the sacrifices in which as principles of action the penitent may express the yearning of his contrite heart to wipe out his sins.

He may accept the punishment incident to his sin. The fitness of God's providential visitations is a mystery that continually baffles the human mind. We cannot always associate the punishment with the sin as accurately as we can link a phenomenon with its cause. We have, in the case of the destruction of Sodom and Gomorrah,[84] visible evidence of God's wrath against sin. But our minds are too limited to impute assertively and with absolute finality a specific motive to God, as we try to unravel the mystery of His providential judgments.

God often uses the chastening rod of pain to increase the virtue of His creatures. "Whom the Lord loveth, He

[84] Gen. 18:20, 19:24-25.

chastiseth, and He scourgeth every son whom He receiveth."[85] Still, the conscience of humanity senses with wondrous accuracy the visitation of God's judgment for particular sins. And Holy Scripture is replete with very definite examples of the just retribution of God falling upon this or that sin of His people.

The thief on the cross is a striking instance of a soul humbly and contritely accepting the punishment of sin in a spirit of loving, wholehearted self-sacrifice. He realized the absolute justice of his end of sorrow and shame. He bore the full burden of the wrath of God. He willingly drained the cup of bitterness that his life of sin had pressed to his lips. His words to the other thief — "Neither dost thou fear God, seeing thou art under the same condemnation? And we indeed justly; for we receive the due reward of our deeds. But this man hath done no evil"[86] — reveal his intense sorrow, his perfect resignation to the divine will through his free acceptance of the full chastisement of the God whom he had forsaken.

With a contrition that words cannot convey, he cries out from the deepest depth of his sinful soul: "Lord,

[85] Heb. 12:6.

[86] Luke 23:40-41.

remember me when Thou shalt come into Thy kingdom."[87] It was a "sorrow according to God" that, moving to mercy the agonized Redeemer, washed away all his sins. "Jesus said to him: 'Amen, I say to thee, this day thou shalt be with me in Paradise.' "[88]

The repentance of Mary Magdalene beautifully illustrates another side of the principle of self-sacrifice. What a life of shameless sin was hers, what indulgence of the flesh, what impure loves, what a prostitution of youth and beauty! Speechless with sorrow, shame, and remorse, she falls on her knees at the feet of Christ — faith, hope, love, and contrition indelibly written on her face. Her eyes, which had made an idol of sinful glances, are flooded with tears of soulful penitence that flow freely down upon the Master's feet. Her hair, whose luxuriant beauty had led so many to yield to the seductive charms of sensuality, falls unregarded over her shoulders as if she expressed by this neglect her profound humiliation and bitter grief; moreover, it is the very towel with which she wipes the feet of her God, bathed by her penitential tears. Her polluted lips she purifies by

[87] Luke 23:42.

[88] Luke 23:43.

pressing them to the virginal flesh of Christ, her heart throbbing with abiding sorrow and undying love.[89]

A new life immediately springs up within her, and henceforth, she is ever at Jesus' side. Her box of precious ointment is a fit symbol of the odor of sanctity emanating from her regenerate soul. She had descended to the depths of moral degradation by her sinful estrangement from Christ; now she ascends the heights of moral heroism. She "loved much,"[90] and like all true lovers, she ever sought the closest union with the God who was the object of her soul's ardor. She would undo the self-desecration of her youth by the permanent dedication of herself and her gifts to God, who had transformed her with His grace.

The principle of self-sacrifice is also exemplified in the diverse urgings of repentance to release and thus lighten the burden of the soul's pent-up energy, or to chastise the offending faculty, the sinful sense, and thus prove the soul's loathing of its past guilt. St. Peter relieved the burning fervor of his repentance by furrowing his cheeks with tears. Enumerating the essentials of

[89] Luke 7:37-38.

[90] Luke 7:47.

this godly sorrow, St. Paul exclaims to the Corinthians, "See what earnestness this godly grief has produced in you, what eagerness to clear yourselves, what indignation, what alarm, what longing, what zeal, what punishment!"[91]

Self-denial in all its complex varieties — special fasting, untiring toil, persevering prayer, constant Christian charity, total forgetfulness of self — all these are the effects of the working of love striving to deepen the soul's hatred of its former shame. Under the inspiration of the soul's consciousness of forgiveness, self-reproachful love yearns to manifest in deed and in truth the sincerity of the soul's unswerving loyalty to Christ, who has so lovingly shown to the soul the fullness of His unspeakable mercy.

There is still another form of the spirit of sacrifice that meets us everywhere, since it is God's obvious ordination. This yoke of penitential discipline God has laid upon every child of the human race. It is the necessary condition of our existence. It is so intimately interwoven with every phase of life that we fail to appreciate it as a distinct punishment ordained by God.

[91] 2 Cor. 7:11 (RSV).

How varied is the penal character of life's journey! Physical pain, mental anxiety, the injustice of our fellowmen, their inconstancy, the irritating features of each day's routine, bitter disappointments, the severing of the dearest ties, shattered ideals, the overbearing demands of gross selfishness — such are the multiple developments of the unfolding of the primeval decree: "Because thou hast hearkened to the voice of thy wife, and hast eaten of the tree whereof I commanded thee that thou shouldst not eat, cursed is the earth in thy work; with labor and toil shalt thou eat thereof all the days of thy life. Thorns and thistles shall it bring forth to thee; and thou shalt eat the herbs of the earth. In the sweat of thy face shalt thou eat bread till thou return to the earth out of which thou wast taken: for dust thou art and into dust thou shalt return."[92]

We live in a fallen world. We must therefore work out our destiny under the conditions created by sin. Did we but realize this truth, we would accept each of life's trying changes in the same spirit in which we accept the penance from the confessor. Were we truly convinced that our hope of pardon, and consequently

[92] Gen. 3:17-19.

our salvation, depend upon repentance, we would willingly undergo all the sufferings of life's warfare.

Every infirmity of our flesh, every cross inflicted upon us by others, every untoward circumstance of our earthly lot, would then be fuel to feed the flames of our penitential love, which, by its reparation of the past, would render our holocaust acceptable to God. The principle of self-sacrifice — love — is always active and inventive. It ever seeks, in every event of life's fitful fever, opportunities to consummate its giving of self.

All, however, cannot attain to the same degree of sacrifice. There are chosen souls whom God has raised above the ordinary callings of life, who, true to their vocation, show their love for God in heroic self-denial, in total surrender to His will, exulting in the use of all their powers to spread His kingdom. But regardless of disparity of calling, all can be led by the same spirit. It is the spirit, not the measure, of sacrifice that will decide our eternity.

The form that our daily cross takes may be one or another or all of these distinct laws of satisfaction, each of which may stand alone, or interchange, or even blend imperceptibly with another. In this way, true repentance seeks to make reparation for past sins; and the more the soul emphasizes in its spiritual life the inexorable law of self-sacrifice, the greater will be its progress in sanctity. In the light of this truth, the sincerely penitent soul, no matter how sinful its past, may reach as high a degree of holiness as the soul that has never lost its baptismal innocence. There are no limits to its spiritual advancement.

This is, indeed, a remarkable instance of the fulfillment of Christ's words: "So shall the last be first and the first last."[93] Grace displays its marvelous efficacy preeminently in a soul whose supreme law is self-sacrifice. The realization of the marked contrast between the past and the present; the consciousness of the miracle of divine mercy wrought where sin prevailed; the sense of the sunshine of God's love dispelling the darkness of sin; the remembrance of the peaceful serenity following absolution, of the irritating oversolicitude swallowed up in humble confidence in God, of the torturing fear driven out by comforting charity, of the past erased, of the faculties of the soul spiritually recreated, so to speak; and the mastering of the infirmities of the flesh that perhaps had reduced the spirit to the level of the brute — such

[93] Matt. 20:16.

are the elements urging the soul to total self-surrender to the divine will, to entire dedication of its life to God. Such a penitent may now attain to heights of holiness never reached even by the soul ever faithful.

But the sanctified soul also may advance still further in the way of God by deep, abiding repentance. With its spiritual vision sharpened to a keener view of its slight sins, and with a finer appreciation of God's patience toward it, despite its faults, under the stimulus of a living consciousness of God's forgiving love — in the depths of such a soul a sense of ardently sincere gratitude will be awakened that will carry the soul to the very apex of sanctity. There is no limit to the virtue to which a soul may attain when ever-deepening repentance keeps pace with growth in holiness.

As an impetus to the development of the penitential spirit, we must remember that we are to "fill up those things that are wanting of the sufferings of Christ, in . . . [our] flesh, for His Body, which is the Church."[94] To do this, we must share in the spirit of His sufferings. To assimilate the sacrificial spirit of Christ is to render His Passion and death eternally efficacious in our souls, to

[94] Col. 1:24.

keep the great commandment of the law. The hope of fulfilling our vocation, of presenting our bodies "a living sacrifice, holy and acceptable to God, which is our spiritual worship,"[95] we will realize only if we are led by His spirit of enduring self-oblation.

In myriad ways we can "fill up those things that are wanting of the sufferings of Christ": by fidelity in the discharge of the ordinary duties of our calling; singleness of purpose sanctifying the performance of our daily actions; the constant striving to compensate for bad example by greater good example; being a peacemaker where we have caused strife and discord; closing the wounds which we have inflicted on others through hatred or envy, by our willingness to spend ourselves and be spent for them in a spirit of charity; thrilling with joy hearts that we have riven with sorrow; saying a word for the cause of Christ, where our cowardliness has betrayed it; foregoing our own wishes and interests, even our just claims, in a spirit of reparation for the disregarded claims and disappointed love of Christ.

And united with the crucified Savior by participation in His Passion, we shall reap our reward for the

[95] Cf. Rom. 12:1 (RSV).

most insignificant act done in His name to the least of His brethren. "Whosoever shall give you to drink a cup of water in my name, because you belong to Christ: Amen, I say to you, he shall not lose his reward."[96] "Amen, I say to you, as long as you did it to one of these my least brethren, you did it to me."[97]

Innumerable and various are God's gifts. "There are diversities of graces, but the same Spirit; and there are diversities of ministries, but the same Lord. And there are diversities of operations, but the same God, who worketh all in all."[98] Bound up with God's gifts are the different powers and opportunities with which He has endowed His creatures, and by means of which He wishes to save them.

It is not our particular calling, but the spirit in which we pursue it, that will crown us eternally. Our great concern, therefore, should be for the inner spirit of sacrifice rather than for the external form which that spirit may embody. Not our vocation, but the humble acceptance and the patient endurance of its hardships, will gain us

[96] Mark 9:40 (RSV = Mark 9:41).

[97] Matt. 25:40.

[98] 1 Cor. 12:4-6.

Heaven. To be animated by the spirit of Christ's life of self-extinction, regardless of the state in which Providence has placed us, constitutes the sacrifice that He expects from us; the free, loving sacrifice for His sake, the sacrifice alone eternally acceptable to Him.

Chapter Six

Resolve to change

"Turn to the Lord,
and forsake thy sins."

Ecclesiasticus 17:25
(RSV= Sirach 17:25)

Amendment of life is the proof of true conversion. Without it, confession and satisfaction are useless. Confession removes the obstacles to the attainment of grace, and the self-sacrifice characteristic of satisfaction is efficacious only when undergone by the soul united to God. Repentance without amendment is mere sentiment. In this instance, nature and grace are strikingly identical.

Some natures are, as a rule, very impressionable, easily moved to devotion, readily touched to tears; but, often, both devotion and tears are the direct results of wounded pride, a balm to subtle self-complacency. So, too, self-denial may be void of suffering, a mere accidental change in our attitude toward sin, implying no real sacrifice, no true foregoing of the free proximate occasions of sin. Repentance of so frail a texture cannot withstand the stress and storm of temptation.

The apparent absence, on the other hand, of supernatural sorrow may beget mistaken fears about the reality of sincere penitence. An earthly reverse may have affected the soul with a keener sensible sorrow than could all the guilt of sin. This is not surprising, because man cannot always control his feelings. He cannot divest himself of nature's instincts, the emotions of his heart. Supernatural sorrow, as sorrow, need not rise above the level of natural sorrow.

Natures are as variant as their sensations. Some cannot conceal their feelings. Others are very calm externally, but internally they are burdened with anguish that is too poignant and deep for expression. If repentance were the result of mere impulse, it would be dependent upon man's baser nature.

Not sensible tenderness, but the firm purpose of amendment is the infallible test of the truth and power of contrition. It differs from every other sorrow by the resoluteness of will, by the rigidly fixed determination of the afflicted heart to turn wholly to God. Its strength is attested by the change in the higher faculties of the soul, which maintain their mastery over sin through the ardently strong faith with which they now cling to God. We do not judge the strength of nature's complex forces by their external noisiness, but by their silent, steady, invisible workings.

In like manner, the secret and unseen resolve of the resolute will, not the variable tenderness of vacillating feelings, is the best criterion that the soul has risen from the death of sin and has, through correspondence with grace, dedicated itself to God. Tears are therefore no genuine evidence of sorrow for sin, because sorrow does not depend upon the impulsive fluctuations of the animal spirits, but upon the self-sacrifice, the self-denial which the spiritually renewed soul is willing to undergo rather than sin again. Such a soul, filled with the joy of wholly undeserved pardon, folds itself more securely than ever in the almighty embrace of God's eternal love.

How comprehensive, how progressive is the soul's thorough conversion from sin to God! The indulgence of passion, the haunts of sin, are abandoned forever; a striking change comes over the soul, for God has effected a new creation within it.

An amended life implies two distinct ideas — one objective, the other subjective. The purpose of amendment involves an internal and an external change. Grace sharpens the soul's eyes the better to behold sin's malice, and strengthens the will to reject what the eyes see so vividly.

Thus, two distinct operations marked David's conversion; with rare condensation of thought does he express these concurrent facts, the subjective and the objective elements in his conversion: "I know my iniquity, and my sin is always before me."[99] His consciousness of his sin was the subjective reality of his changed life, the free correspondence of his will with grace, whose strong energies rendered him again acceptable to God. The sin ever before him was the objective reality.

Every true conversion is the same. Spiritual apprehension is quickened, the scales fall from the eyes of the soul, and the misguided will emerges from the darkness and slavery of sin into the light and liberty of the children of God. A new world has been opened up to the sinner, in which he ascends from grace to grace, from virtue to virtue.

Wondrous, indeed, is this new world into which the soul has entered after having rid itself of sin. The keen vision of God's mercy, His unspeakable patience, His eternal love, His infinite purity, the miracles of His grace, the mysterious workings of His Providence, and the sublime efficacy of prayer now appeal to the soul

[99] Ps. 50:5 (RSV = Ps. 51:3).

with indescribable power. Deeply conscious of its intimate union with God, the soul, in the freshness of its spiritual regeneration and urged by grace, advances rapidly in Christian perfection, constantly discovering new ways of progressing in virtue.

All is changed. The barren waste of sin is now a garden redolent of delicious spiritual fragrance; light disperses the darkness, illumines the perplexing mysteries of life, irradiates sorrow and suffering, even death, and compels them to proclaim with divine eloquence the marvels of infinite mercy and eternal love. God has made all things new.

This newness of life awakens in the soul a better appreciation of the spiritual. It strengthens faith and raises the soul to a higher level where, touched with grace, the soul cooperates all the more readily and easily with it, and more vividly apprehends the wisdom that "reacheth from end to end mightily and ordereth all things sweetly."[100]

Thus does God draw souls to Him. He cleanses the soul's eyes to see the truth and — under the realization of the soul's spiritual renewal and nobler ideals — to

[100]Wisd. 8:1.

grasp it and to conform to the divine will on a higher plane of holiness.

This law of grace is a necessary impetus to quicken the faith of the penitent, and so to prepare him, by inspiring him with unfaltering hope, for the miracle of compassion that God is about to work in his conversion. In the heart of the sinner, the appreciation of God's mercy is very weak and fitful. His spiritual apprehension is dulled by the constant commission of sin, and although at times he yearns to be virtuous, too often, frightened by imaginary hindrances, he stifles his longing and remains the victim of complex, sinful self-indulgence. Like a traveler in total darkness, his soul sorely needs the light from the illuminated mountain of God to enable him to rise from sin to virtue, through his free acceptance of the divine mercy.

This law is the groundwork of the practical teachings of Holy Scripture. We work with God according to the measure of our appreciation of the quickening power of His grace. Such is the soul of the psalmist's beautiful exhortation: "Cast thy care upon the Lord, and He shall sustain thee."[101] We fulfill the duties of our state in life

[101] Ps. 54:23 (RSV = Ps. 55:22).

with the highest spiritual efficiency in proportion to the strength of our faith in the wondrous effects of grace, as manifested by our wholehearted correspondence with it.

From its birth until its full maturity in the soul, the spiritual life admits of three stages of development — the purgative, the illuminative, and the unitive — harmonizing, respectively, with the three great mysteries in Christ's life: His circumcision, His baptism, and His Ascension. Like the creature in all things save sin, Christ's own life thus parallels the progressive spiritual advancement of the renewed powers of man's nature.

Christ's circumcision revealed the fact that man's nature was in Him completely purified. His baptism was the further development of His human nature through the divine enlightenment of the Holy Spirit. His human nature attained its meridian splendor when, having ascended into Heaven, it was enthroned at the right hand of the Father. The progress of the spiritual renewal of the soul, if inferior in degree and imperfect, corresponds truly and in kind to these developments in the life of God incarnate.

These three different stages of the penitential life do not alternate with mathematical precision. One does not cease and another begin. They may so intermingle that no sharp distinction can be drawn between them. One may even revert to the other, and none of them is ever perfect in this life. No matter how far man may advance in any of them, he never loses his imperfection.

Nonetheless, certain characteristics distinguish them from one another. In the order of their succession also, and in their progressive development, one rises higher than the other.

The first stage of true repentance is necessarily purgative. It begins with the struggle against sin. The washing away of past sins, the persevering effort against bad thoughts and evil desires, the suppression of anger, the mortification of the sensual appetite, the conquest of covetousness, hatred, jealousy, and selfishness in its diversified shapes and forms — purgation is the first step in the penitential life, the moral circumcision of the sinner's soul, in union with the mystery of Christ's physical circumcision.

Having gained the victory, joyously alive in its spiritual rebirth, strong with the strength of God, the soul presses forward, growing in wisdom unto sobriety and advancing in holiness by peace of mind under pain, tranquillity in trial, meekness in humiliation, forbearance under gross injustice, and a more religious response to the truths of their Faith. In short, the soul is enriched, like the glorious human soul of Christ in His baptism, with the illumination of the Holy Spirit, which wholly scatters the dense darkness of sin.

But the soul has not yet reached the fullness of its spiritual development. There is a still greater power of expansion in its renewed life. It attains to the highest holiness if it strives, with all its power, under the tremendous influence of grace, to will what God wills, to make God the center from which all its thoughts, words, and deeds radiate and to which they all converge; to prefer the glory of God before all things; to seek, in everything, to be hidden with Christ in God; to be lost in Him, and to be one with Him. Like Christ in His Ascension, the soul ascends spiritually to its divine Lover, to rest forever in Him.

Definiteness is the touchstone of the truth and the strength of practical amendment. The universally applicable test of an amended life is not the mere conquest of a ruling passion, but the development of its opposite virtue. Mary Magdalene luminously illustrates this truth. Her early life was the apotheosis of carnal self-indulgence. All she was and had were dedicated to sin. Touched by grace, she so disciplined herself that no sacrifice was too great if she might be forever united with the God from whom she had been so rudely and completely torn by the reign of passion.

So true was her fidelity, so unalterable her affection, that neither the horrors of the Cross nor the terrors of the sepulcher could separate her from Him. Doubtless realizing, in her deep diffidence of self, the sad plight of her former life without God, she yearned, after her conversion, to preclude the possibility of again living without Him, even if it might cost her her life.

St. Peter is another notable example of this complete conversion. How rashly vaunting, how impulsively self-reliant he was! Correspondence with grace taught him, as nothing else could, that man left to himself is "wretched and miserable and poor and blind and naked."[102]

Absolute distrust of self is therefore the dominant and refreshing note of St. Peter's letters. "Be sober," he says, "and watch, because your adversary the Devil, as a roaring lion, goeth about seeking whom he may devour."[103] "Be humbled therefore under the mighty hand of God, that He may exalt you in the time of visitation;

[102]Rev. 3:17.

[103]1 Pet. 5:8.

casting all your care upon Him, for He hath care of you."[104] "Be prudent therefore, and watch in prayers."[105] "Insinuate humility one to another, for God resisteth the proud, but to the humble He giveth grace."[106]

Accordingly, then, as we supplant our besetting sin with its opposite virtue, accordingly as anger gives place to meekness, and self-indulgence to self-denial and self-sacrifice; accordingly as, where we were inordinately self-assertive, we are truly, even though very slowly, becoming more distrustful of ourselves. Briefly, accordingly as we conquer sin with the triumphant power of grace, we may be certain of the truth and reality of our conversion. The mighty power of Hell has been broken by the mightier power of Heaven.

Humility is another test also universally applicable. When the natural instinct of self-complacency ceases to rule us, when we so master ourselves as to become lowly and mean in our own eyes and not to hanker after the praises of our fellowmen, we are turning to God, heart and soul. Pride was the cause, not the effect, of

[104] 1 Pet. 5:6, 7.

[105] 1 Pet. 4:7.

[106] 1 Pet. 5:5.

man's loss of supernatural righteousness. It is therefore bone of our bones and flesh of our flesh.[107] Anger, avarice, envy, and all the other sins flow from Original Sin. Pride was the Fall.

We must realize the fact in order to understand how deeply this vice is rooted in us. Prior to all other evils, it abides as the stimulus to them all. To counteract this evil, Christ descended to the depths of humility. His lowliness was to be a constant contradiction of man's first and most frequent sin.

Why did Christ suffer and die? "Christ died for all: that they also who live may not now live to themselves, but unto Him who died for them and rose again."[108] Emphasizing Christ's characteristic quality, St. Augustine would have Him say to us: "Learn of me, not to create the world, not to call out of nothing the visible and the invisible, not to work miracles in the world and to raise the dead, but to be meek and humble of heart."[109]

There is not and there never can be any amendment without humility. We are truly converted only when we

[107]Gen. 2:23.

[108]2 Cor. 5:15.

[109]St. Augustine, Sermon 10.

repeatedly sacrifice ourselves, in the ever-deepening conviction of our nothingness, not fitfully, but perseveringly, until death, so that Christ may live in us.

For the progressive development of amendment is coextensive with our earthly existence, to become perfect only when we shall have realized our supernatural destiny. In the true realization of an amended life, our desires must expand to the unlimited possibilities of which the perfect man developed by God "unto the measure of the age of the fullness of Christ"[110] will hereafter be the recipient. The boundless capacities of our spiritual renewal in the world to come should therefore sustain us and urge us onward when we become discouraged and dispirited by our failure to advance more rapidly here on earth.

Our striving after the ideal here, and its realization hereafter, constitute our moral greatness. Not our actual attainment of perfection now, but our progress toward its future acquisition, is the measure of our moral worth. The possibilities of grace cannot be gauged by any earthly standard. During our exile, we cannot imitate Christ perfectly. Our perfection now is "in part": "We

[110]Eph. 4:13.

know in part, and we prophesy in part. But when that which is perfect is come, that which is in part shall be done away."[111]

The great apostle enforces this truth: "Brethren, I do not count myself to have apprehended. But one thing I do: forgetting the things that are behind and stretching forth myself to those that are before, I press toward the mark, to the prize of the supernal vocation of God in Christ Jesus."[112] We test our religious strength by its possibility rather than by its reality. The present is indicative of the future. As the twig is inclined, so shall it grow. God is invisible, but the visible within our grasp leads to Him. The way to perfection is open to us. God at its end is hidden from our eyes.

Stunted in spiritual growth, we struggle in this perishable life, striving to develop to full stature, like the rosebud struggling under the chilling frost of ungenial skies to expand to perfect proportions. The same law inspires the hope that the weak but earnest efforts of our souls here, far from God, and consequently crippled and halted in their spiritual progress by the criminal cravings

[111] 1 Cor. 13:9-10.

[112] Phil. 3:13-14.

of the flesh, will attain their full strength and be crowned with the crown of eternal success when we behold God "face-to-face,"[113] and "shall be like to Him because we shall see Him as He is."[114]

Our salvation depends more on hope than on its fruition here. We are saved more by faith increasing, tendencies developing, and charity expanding than by knowledge acquired, results obtained, and victories won. We can only measure our movements onward and watch their direction, but never compass their full possibilities. Our pursuit of holiness, not its actual acquisition, is the basis of our judgment of the extent of our virtue. Like wayfarers, we are more concerned with the signs along our route than with the completion of our journey.

All therefore is well, and there is no need of vacuity and depression of soul over the littleness of our amendment, if we are corresponding with grace, and thus gradually forming and fashioning Christ within us. We are growing in virtue imperceptibly, just as the tender seedling, in its predestined vigorous fullness, slowly expands into flower.

[113] 1 Cor. 13:12.

[114] 1 John 3:2.

But we must never forget that life is a time of trial. One very fundamental law of the mystery of our probation, one law that greatly elucidates the many perplexing phenomena of life, one primary law of spiritual progress, St. Paul states very tersely: "What things a man shall sow, those also shall he reap."[115]

Here, we are partakers of God's mercy, so rich in patience, so persistently forbearing, so lovingly forgiving. Hereafter, justice will insist on its own rigorous claims which God will reconcile completely with the benefactions of His mercy. Only the pure of heart will then see God; only the just will then shine in the Sun of eternal justice.[116] The joy of the soul that was sinless is not the keenest and most thrilling joy of Paradise. The tears of penitents, the diamonds of Heaven's dome, beget the highest joy before the angels of God — the joy with which they ever exult.

"There shall be joy in Heaven upon one sinner that doth penance, more than upon ninety-nine just who need not penance."[117] The abiding consciousness of the

[115]Gal. 6:8.

[116]Matt. 5:8, 13:43.

[117]Luke 15:7.

Hell from which they have been delivered, the wholly undeserved mercy that wrought their deliverance, the astounding contrast of the possibility of their endless misery with the actual attainment of their unending happiness as they are lost in God, constitute the supreme ecstasy of the souls whose penitential sorrow has been changed into everlasting joy. The realization of their past sin is the measure of their perfect possession of enduring bliss. Corroding anxieties and agonizing doubts yield to tranquil peace and calm certainty; soothing rest has succeeded feverish toil; the night is past forever; the eternal day has dawned.

Appendix

How to make a good confession

Elements of a Good Confession

- *Examine your conscience* to recall sins or faults you committed since your last good confession. Making a daily examination of conscience will better help you conquer your sins. (See page 114 for a comprehensive examination of conscience that may help you.)

- *Be sorry for your sins, and resolve not to sin again* (see Chapter 3).

- *Confess your sins* honestly and completely to a priest. For mortal sins, you must confess the sin, as well as the number of times you committed it, to the best of your recollection. If you forget a sin, your confession will still be valid, but you should confess the sin the next time you make a confession. You should not fail to mention to the priest any serious sins of which you are aware. It is not necessary to confess venial sins, although doing so will help you overcome them. Mention or ask about anything you are unsure about.

• Listen to the advice the priest gives you, pray an act of contrition (see page 112 for examples), and *fulfill the penance* the priest assigns you.

Steps for Confession
for Roman Catholics

• Enter the confessional and kneel (or sit for a face-to-face confession).

• Make the Sign of the Cross, and then say, "Forgive me, Father, for I have sinned. It has been [mention interval] since my last confession. These are my sins."

• Confess your sins. You must confess all mortal sins you have committed, to the best of your recollection, and any venial sins you wish to confess. When you have finished confessing your sins, say, "For these and for all my sins I am very sorry."

• The priest may ask you about any part of your confession that he may not have understood, and he may offer you counsel and guidance regarding the sins you confessed. He will then assign you a penance — often prayers to say or good works to perform.

• Pray an act of contrition (see next page for examples). Often the priest will invite you to do so.

• The priest will then say the prayer of absolution: "God, the Father of mercies, through the death and resurrection of His Son has reconciled the world to Himself and sent the Holy Spirit among us for the forgiveness of sins; through the ministry of the Church, may God give you pardon and peace, and I absolve you from your sins in the name of the Father, and of the Son, and of the Holy Spirit." Respond, "Amen."

• The priest will then dismiss you and may say, "Go in peace" or "God bless you." Respond, "Thank you, Father," and leave the confessional.

Three Acts of Contrition

O my God,
I am heartily sorry
for having offended Thee,
and I detest all my sins
because I dread the loss of Heaven
and the pains of Hell,
but most of all because I have
offended Thee, my God,
who are all good and
deserving of all my love.
I firmly resolve,
with the help of Thy grace,
to confess my sins, to do penance,
and to amend my life. Amen.

O my God,
I am heartily sorry
for having offended Thee,
and I detest all my sins
because of Thy just punishments,

but most of all because
they offend Thee, my God,
who are all good
and deserving of all my love.
I firmly resolve,
with the help of Thy grace,
to sin no more and to avoid
the near occasions of sin. Amen.

My God,
I am sorry for my sins
with all my heart.
In choosing to do wrong and
in failing to do good,
I have sinned against Thee,
whom I should love above all things.
I firmly intend, with Your help,
to do penance, to sin no more,
and to avoid whatever leads to sin.
Our Savior Jesus Christ
suffered and died for us.
In His name, my God,
have mercy. Amen.

Examination of Conscience

As you prepare for Confession, these questions may help you to examine how faithfully you have lived according to the Ten Commandments.

"I am the Lord, your God.
You shall have no other gods
besides me."

Have I doubted God's existence?

Have I been ungrateful to God for His benefits?

Do I try to hide from God because I love my sin or because I do not have strength of will to make sacrifices for His sake?

Have I failed to give God the respect, the love, and the simplicity of a child toward his Father?

Am I unwilling to cast out and destroy everything that makes my soul unworthy to be the dwelling place of the three divine Persons?

Have I grumbled against God's will?

Do I refuse to accept troubles that come to me as a means of salvation?

Do I trouble others with my grievances?

Have I ignored Christ's voice within my soul when He has asked me for some sacrifice?

Do I lack peace of soul because I don't trust God?

Have I been too proud to accept well-merited correction, even from my confessor?

Do I rely solely on myself and not on God?

Do I neglect my duties as a creature to my Creator?

Do I have an exaggerated fear of death? Do I trustfully abandon my past to God's mercy and my future to His love?

Have I abandoned the Catholic Faith?

Have I joined a non-Catholic church?

Have I refused to believe any truths of the Faith or any teachings of the Church?

Did I fail to profess or defend the Faith when required to do so?

Have I ridiculed the teachings or practices of the Church?

Have I destroyed or lessened the faith of others by speaking contemptuously about religion, the Church, priests, and so forth?

Am I ashamed of my Faith in front of others?

Did I read materials or associate with people who might endanger my faith?

Am I a member of a society or organization that is opposed to the Church?

Have I attended or taken part in the marriage of a Catholic in a wedding not approved by the Church?

Have I neglected my Easter duty — that is, have I failed to receive Holy Communion at least once between Easter and Trinity Sunday?

Have I failed to go to Confession at least once a year?

Did I fail to carry out the penance assigned to me in a past confession?

Did I neglect to fast and to abstain from eating meat on days when I was required to do so?

Have I been inattentive during prayer? Have I willingly entertained distractions?

Have I been unfaithful to daily prayer?

Have I received Holy Communion without reverence? Have I neglected to make a proper thanksgiving after receiving?

Do I fail to examine my conscience regularly and often?

Am I ignorant of any of the commandments or teachings of the Church? Have I failed to instruct myself further in the Faith?

Do I neglect to read Scripture?

Do I omit my religious exercises or put them off for no good reason?

Do I let my religious practices annoy others?

Do I neglect to try to correct myself, remembering that I should always strive for perfection?

Have I fully intended to commit sin, even though I may not have successfully accomplished the act?

Have I evaded an opportunity to enlighten someone on religious truth?

"You shall not take the name of the Lord, your God, in vain."

Do I speak blasphemously about God, Jesus, Mary, the angels, or the saints?

Do I use God's name carelessly, in anger, or in surprise?

Do I speak irreverently of holy persons, places, or things?

Have I called down evil upon anyone or anything?

"Remember the Sabbath Day, to keep it holy."

Did I miss Mass on a Sunday or on a holy day of obligation through my own fault?

Did I arrive at Mass late or leave early without good reason?

Do I allow myself to be distracted during Mass?

Have I done unnecessary servile work or conducted business on Sunday?

"Honor your father and your mother."

Have I disobeyed, insulted, or shown disrespect to my parents, grandparents, guardians, or superiors?

Am I disrespectful, impolite, or discourteous toward my family?

Have I failed to have my children baptized or receive First Communion or Confirmation?

Do I fail to educate my children in the Faith?

Have I failed to take my children to Mass on Sundays and on holy days of obligation?

Have I failed to meet my children's physical, spiritual, emotional, and educational needs?

Do I mistreat, belittle, or abuse my children?

Have I failed to care for and provide for my parents in time of need?

Have I neglected the duties of my state of life?

Have I disobeyed the lawful demands of my superiors, teachers, or employer?

Have I neglected my work or my studies?

Am I disrespectful toward the elderly?

Am I disobedient to the civil law or to those in authority?

Do I fail to pray daily for my parents, my family, and my benefactors?

"You shall not kill."

Have I murdered anyone or killed anyone through negligence or carelessness?

Did I perform or assist in an abortion?

Did I have an abortion?

Did I force, pressure, or mislead a woman into having an abortion?

Have I participated in surrogate motherhood?

Have I received or participated in artificial insemination?

Have I been surgically sterilized?

Have I mutilated my body or another's body?

Did I attempt suicide?

Do I act violently?

Have I needlessly put my life or others' lives in danger?

Have I driven recklessly or carelessly?

Did I strike or fight with another?

Do I drink alcohol excessively or smoke excessively?

Do I abuse prescribed drugs?

Do I use, distribute, or sell illegal drugs?

Do I eat too much or sleep too much?

Do I endanger my health by eating too little or sleeping too little?

Do I neglect my health?

Am I too concerned about my health or my appearance?

Do I fail to wish my neighbor all the good things that I wish for myself?

Do I deliberately harbor unkind and revengeful thoughts about others?

Have I taken revenge?

Have I attributed bad motives to others, when I could not be certain of their motives?

Have I used harsh or abusive language toward another?

Am I rude, impolite, or inconsiderate?

Do I ridicule others?

As a husband or wife, have I failed prudently to make an effort to prevent the sins of my spouse?

Have I neglected my duty of preventing those in my charge from committing sin, or correcting them after they have failed?

Have I failed to report to an appropriate authority actions that are harmful to the innocent or to the community?

After a quarrel, have I refused to make efforts at reconciliation?

Do I set bad examples for others?

Have I failed to help someone in danger or in need?

Am I stubborn in my opinions?

Do I disagree with Church teachings on abortion, sterilization, and contraception?

Am I impatient?

Am I cruel to animals?

Have I failed to show respect to my social inferiors as children of God?

Have I spread gloom by giving way to morose and sullen moods?

Do I habitually look for flaws and point them out to others?

Do I put a damper on others' joys by my negative attitude?

Do I complain?

Have I made cutting and sarcastic remarks to others?

Have I cooperated with another in committing a sin?

When I had the opportunity, have I done nothing to prevent evil?

Have I led others into sin by suggestion or bad example?

Do I guard my words and conduct, especially when in the presence of children?

Have I permitted someone to suffer injustice or mistreatment when I could have prevented it?

Do I hurt others by my anger and impatience?

Do I lead others into venial sin by unreasonably teasing or annoying them?

Have I dissuaded another person from doing a good work?

"You shall not commit adultery."
"You shall not covet your neighbor's wife."

Have I committed fornication?

Have I committed adultery?

Have I aroused illicit sexual desire in myself or another by impure passionate kissing, embracing, or touching?

Do I masturbate?

Do I engage in homosexual acts?

Do I use artificial contraceptives or other birth-prevention methods forbidden by the Church?

Have I refused my spouse the marriage right without a good reason or made an unreasonable demand for it?

Am I dating someone who is civilly divorced but is still bound by a valid marriage?

Do I dress immodestly?

Have I entertained impure thoughts or desires?

Have I read impure material, listened to music with impure lyrics, or looked at impure images, whether in pictures or on television or on videotape?

Do I use vulgar language or tell or listen to impure jokes or stories?

Do I associate with people of immoral character who are or may be occasions of sin?

"You shall not steal."

Have I stolen money or property?

Have I failed to make restitution for what I stole?

Have I damaged property?

Have I accepted or bought stolen property?

Have I helped someone steal?

Have I smuggled goods?

Did I file an unjust lawsuit or make unjust claims in a lawsuit?

Am I dishonest in my business dealings?

As a merchant, have I charged unreasonably high prices or intentionally hidden the defects of the items I sell?

Do I fail to pay workers a just amount?

Have I failed to do the amount of work for which I am paid? Have I been careless in my work?

Do I neglect to pay income tax?

Have I neglected to pay my debts?

Am I incurring debts that I shall never be able to repay?

Have I bribed someone or accepted a bribe?

Do I gamble excessively?

Have I borrowed something without the owner's permission?

Have I failed to return something I borrowed?

Do I waste money or spend it extravagantly?

Have I squandered money and thus left my family in want of necessary things?

Do I waste goods or food?

Do I neglect to give to the Church as my means allow?

Have I refused to give alms for the relief of the needy or to charitable causes, even though I had opportunities and sufficient means to do so?

Have I cheated on tests or schoolwork?

Have I cheated in games or sports?

Have I been stingy with my time, money, and talents?

"You shall not bear false witness against your neighbor."

Have I lied deliberately?

Have I lied under oath?

Have I failed to keep vows or oaths?

Have I sworn to do something sinful or illegal?

Have I deliberately tried to overhear another's confession?

Have I, by silence or approval, failed to prevent the defamation of another's character when I could have done so?

Have I slandered others by attributing to them sins they did not commit or of which I had no evidence?

Have I discussed or listened to discussions of others' faults?

Have I revealed anyone's secret sins to those who could not otherwise have known them and who had no claim to such information?

Have I caused ill will by telling my friends the unkind remarks others made about them?

Have I told a secret I was asked to keep?

Have I betrayed someone's trust?

Have I read someone else's letters or private documents that I had no right to read?

Have I boasted of my sins?

Have I criticized anyone uncharitably?

Do I make rash judgments and harbor false suspicions about others?

Have I deliberately misled or deceived anyone?

Have I refused to forgive someone or held a grudge against him?

Have I failed to apologize or make amends to someone I offended?

"You shall not covet anything that is your neighbor's."

Am I greedy?

Am I selfish?

Do I indulge in self-pity?

Am I proud?

Am I vain?

Do I desire to be praised?

Do I show off?

Have I exaggerated my success?

Have I minimized or explained away my failures?

In my spirituality, do I seek mere personal excellence?

Have I refused responsibility for fear that it might reveal my limitations?

Have I measured my charity only by what others have given, instead of by my ability to give and by the need of others?

Have I demanded publicity and praise for my almsgiving?

Am I touchy and hypersensitive?

Do I magnify the least oversight or thoughtlessness into an insult or deliberate slight?

Am I envious of someone's possessions, talents, or blessings?

Do I take delight in others' misfortunes?

Biographical Note

John A. Kane

(1883-1962)

Born in Philadelphia, John Kane attended St. Mary's Seminary in Baltimore, Maryland, and St. Charles Borromeo Seminary in Overbrook, Pennsylvania, and was ordained for the Archdiocese of Philadelphia in 1912.

Deeply devoted to the Holy Eucharist, Fr. Kane was the first pastor in his archdiocese to introduce all-night adoration of the Blessed Sacrament. He placed great importance on Catholic education of the young and also sought to educate adults in their Faith, initiating a weekly adult religion class in his parish.

Fr. Kane was known during his lifetime for his great love of prayer and meditation, and his several books give proof of the wisdom gleaned from so many hours of contemplation. His writings bespeak a profound love of Christ and a warm understanding of the Catholic layman's struggle to achieve holiness. His words offer Catholics practical insight and encouragement to seek a deeper union and friendship with God.

Sophia Institute

Sophia Institute is a nonprofit institution that seeks to nurture the spiritual, moral, and cultural life of souls and to spread the Gospel of Christ in conformity with the authentic teachings of the Roman Catholic Church.

Sophia Institute Press fulfills this mission by offering translations, reprints, and new publications that afford readers a rich source of the enduring wisdom of mankind.

Sophia Institute also operates two popular online Catholic resources: CrisisMagazine.com and CatholicExchange.com.

Crisis Magazine provides insightful cultural analysis that arms readers with the arguments necessary for navigating the ideological and theological minefields of the day. *Catholic Exchange* provides world news from a Catholic perspective as well as daily devotionals and articles that will help you to grow in holiness and live a life consistent with the teachings of the Church.

In 2013, Sophia Institute launched Sophia Institute for Teachers to renew and rebuild Catholic culture through service to Catholic education. With the goal of nurturing the spiritual, moral, and cultural life of souls, and an abiding respect for the role and work of teachers, we strive to provide materials and programs that are at once enlightening to the mind and ennobling to the heart; faithful and complete, as well as useful and practical.

Sophia Institute gratefully recognizes the Solidarity Association for preserving and encouraging the growth of our apostolate over the course of many years. Without their generous and timely support, this book would not be in your hands.

www.SophiaInstitute.com
www.CatholicExchange.com
www.CrisisMagazine.com
www.SophiaInstituteforTeachers.org